S0-BJG-918

WITHDRAWN

914.248
Sh1

65861

DATE DUE			
Sep 29 70			

GAYLORD M-2

PRINTED IN U.S.A.

SHAKESPEARE'S
COUNTRY
in Pictures

THE SHAKESPEARE MONUMENT, STRATFORD

SHAKESPEARE'S memory is green eternally in the hearts of men; and every performance of his plays in the theatres of the world celebrates him anew, albeit sometimes less than worthily. "This powerful rhyme" is indeed his enduring memorial. But Stratford's "gilded monuments" include the graceful seated figure, in bronze, designed and presented to the town by Lord Ronald Sutherland Gower. First erected in the Memorial Theatre Gardens in 1888, it was removed some years ago to its present site near Clopton Bridge.

SHAKESPEARE'S
COUNTRY
in Pictures

FOREWORD AND INTRODUCTIONS BY J. C. TREWIN
ILLUSTRATIONS DESCRIBED BY PHILIP CLEAVE

CONTENTS

*

ODHAMS PRESS LTD.   LONG ACRE, LONDON

CARL A. RUDISILL LIBRARY
LENOIR RHYNE COLLEGE

STRATFORD-UPON-AVON

How pre-eminently is Stratford fitted to be the setting for a festival will be plain from this aerial view. Its feature is the Avon, tracing a sinuous course past meadow and garden, whilst Holy Trinity Church—its graceful proportions finely revealed from the air—the Memorial Theatre (behind the poplars), and the two bridges are also prominent. The nearer is the so-called Tramway Bridge; upstream from it is Clopton Bridge. Behind the theatre appear the Bancroft Gardens and, just beyond the basin of the old Stratford canal, now disused, the garden containing the Shakespeare Monument by Gower.

914.248
Sh 1

65861
April 1969

4

Foreword

THERE is, in *Paradise Lost*, a description of how the architect Mulciber was thrown from the battlements of heaven and how

> *From morn*
> *To noon he fell, from noon to dewy eve,*
> *A summer's day.*

It may seem odd to quote Milton, rather than Shakespeare, at the beginning of a record of the Shakespeare Country; but the phrase, in its suggestion of the long hours of midsummer, has always held for me the very spirit of this Midland world in which Shakespeare was bred. One thinks of a hot morning sun scattering the mist along an Avon reach; of the calm, untroubled day, in its descent towards an unsullied evening; of great oaks casting their shade; of Warwickshire water-music; and the view from, say, Sunrising Hill at sunset across the carpet of the Midland plain. It always surprises me that Mulciber "dropped from the zenith, like a falling star" on Lemnos, the Aegean isle. He should have landed in a wide meadow not far from Clopton Bridge, at the core of Shakespeare's Stratford, where the river is bent like a bow. Here at Stratford, within half a mile or so, we have the house in which Shakespeare was born during April, 1564, the school where he was educated, the church in which he is buried, and the theatre in which his works are acted.

I have lived in Stratford-upon-Avon in autumn, when the last leaves have ceased to patter in Holy Trinity churchyard; and in winter when the world's most famous "shrine" is simply a market-town lapped in quiet among the river-pastures. Yet I think always of Stratford and of Warwickshire as a place in which late spring and high summer mingle.

I know that modern traffic prevents us from recommending any main road as a haunt of ancient peace. But in the Warwickshire villages, and on the fringes of Warwickshire and Gloucestershire and Oxfordshire, among these silver-slipping rivers, these burdened trees, these old manors, we do get the feeling that time stands still. "Who stays it still withal?" "With lawyers in the vacation; for they sleep between term and term, and then they perceive not how time moves." That is Rosalind speaking. About lawyers we can only take her word; we know that time stands still in the Shakespeare Country, the pastoral heart of England.

This is not spectacular scenery in the sense that it is wild and strange, with the strangeness of Cornwall or the wildness of the Pennine upland. It is, as someone

Shakespeare's Country

Old Cro...
Meride...

BIRMINGHAM

Hampton-
in-Arden

Solihull

Know...

Packwoo...

Henley-
in-
Arden

Henley-in-
Arden

River Avon

WAR W

WORCESTER

Snitterfield

Wilmcot...

Alcester

Grafton Flyford   Wixford   Stratford-upon-
Bidford   Avon

Pershore
Abbey

VALE OF

Welford

Pershore

Norton
Fladbury

R. Avon

Cropthorne

EVESHAM

Eckington
Elmley Castle

Evesham

Chipping
Campden

Wickhamford

BREDON
HILL

Broadway

Mary Arden's Cottage,
Wilmcote

COTSWOLD

HILLS

FOSSE WAY

GLOUCESTER

Dove-cot,
Hillborough

Alcester

West Gate, Warwick

Meriden

Coventry

Balsall

Rugby

Stoneleigh

River Avon

nilworth

Dunchurch

ys

Leamington

Long
Itchington

ffe

Warwick

Sulgrave
Manor

R. Cherwell

FOSSE WAY

Barford

Ufton

arlecote

Harbury

Kenilworth
Castle

K

Gaydon

Barford

Compton Verney

NORTHANTS

kley

Kineton

tington

EDGE
HILL

ton

Horntou

hipston-

Compton

n-Stour

Wynyates

Barcheston

Brailes

OXON

Sulgrave

ng
mpton

Holy Trinity Church,
Stratford

nne
Hathaway's
Cottage,
Shottery

Gordon Randall

has said, English plain-song. But it has manifold delights, the gentler, pastoral delights. Although the hills may not be very high, you can usually count on enchanting views from them. The rivers may not be very broad, but they have a habit of sliding away into unknown worlds. And the great houses and the small cottages, whether in Cotswold stone or in timber-framing, have a special graciousness and quality.

The old kingdom of Mercia is the very centre of the English scene. We know instinctively, after living in the Shakespeare Country, that William Shakespeare, the Stratford man, must have written the plays attributed to him. The spirit of the area chimes with the Shakespearean verse. When I think of it I think of Masefield's phrase that "life took thought for Shakespeare," breeding him, mind and bone, "in a two-fold district of hill and valley, where country life was at its best, and the beauty of England at its bravest." And I think of special things: the cobweb-grey wraith, the phantom, of the medieval Guild Chapel in the middle of Stratford; the sight of the tall towers of Warwick Castle, emblems of baronial England, above the Avon; the deer-cropped parkland of Charlecote; the tapestried, formalized, green-and-silver stretch of the Midland plain from Edge Hill; the roofs and chimneys of Compton Wynyates in rose-red brick; the decorum of Leamington Spa; the sense of the past at Evesham, where Simon de Montfort fell.

Always for me the Shakespeare Country is in the light of a summer's day. It would be wrong to say that it never rains here, or that in season Warwickshire is free from icicles by the wall or milk that comes frozen home in pail. But in the mind it lies under the sun of late June. I can feel the heat stored in the rose- and plum- and cedar-coloured brickwork, feel the silky-tough texture of riverside grass, see laden trees that might have come from a water-colour by De Wint, hear the clack-and-plash as a rowing-boat thrusts up the Avon into some unexpected glade that seems never to have been explored by man.

There is a constellation of villages (Hampton Lucy, Cleeve Prior, Wilmcote, go where you will), but only four major towns: Stratford-upon-Avon, which is dedicated to Shakespeare; Evesham, which for all its market-bustle appears likely to start back to the Middle Ages at a word; Warwick, which hangs like ivy about the vast castle; and Leamington, in which for me it is a mid-morning coffee-time, an eleven o'clock shopping-hour.

The thing always to be remembered in the Shakespeare Country is that this is Middle England. Henry James said once: "There is no better way for the stranger who wishes to know something of England than to spend a fortnight in Warwickshire. It is the core and centre of the English world . . . unmitigated England." How right the use of that epithet, "unmitigated"! And it is, moreover, an England of the summer, from morn to noon, from noon to dewy eve, a summer's day.　　　　　　　　　　　　　　　　　　　　J. C. TREWIN.

THE SHAKESPEARE HOTEL, WITH THE TOWN HALL BEYOND

INCORPORATING an old timbered mansion called the Five Gables, the Shakespeare Hotel, in Chapel Street, presents a most striking façade. The Town Hall, standing on the site of the former Market Hall built in 1633, dates from 1768. It was dedicated to the memory of Shakespeare by the great David Garrick at the Jubilee celebrations held in the following year.

CLOPTON BRIDGE AND THE AVON

THIS solid structure was built in the reign of Henry VII, under the direction of Sir Hugh Clopton. The arches are fourteen in number, and the joints between the stones give foothold to a surprising number of wallflowers. Visitors of inquiring mind, with a taste for history and detective fiction, may amuse themselves by deciding which of the arches are the two broken down during the Civil War. In 1642 uncertainty as to whether King or Parliament would win the Battle of Edge Hill led to the bridge being prudently rendered unusable.

Stratford and the
Villages

STRATFORD, in the pastoral south-western corner of Warwickshire, is "upon Avon"—Shakespeare's Will calls it "upon"—and we think naturally of the river as the heart of the little town. The very name comes from the Roman road or *straet* across the ford of the Avon. Actually we do not see the river when we are in the main streets; but we have only to walk downhill—down Bridge Street, down Sheep Street, or down Chapel Lane—and there it is at the foot, the current that "with gentle murmur glides," the Avon in its bow between the two bridges and the Collegiate Church of the Holy Trinity.

Anyone who goes to Stratford simply as a shrine-walker will not see much of the Avon, except by the church where the view from the river wall of that calm water and the green-brocaded meadows beyond it is as soothing as we can find in a day's march. Most of the Shakespeare haunts are set back from the river. Thus the Birthplace, rather self-consciously the Birthplace but pleasing to readily responsive spirits, is up in Henley Street. The Grammar School and the lovely ghost of the medieval Guild Chapel are in the centre of the town—one long street, called by three names during its course, runs across Stratford—and here, too, is the site of New Place, the house where Shakespeare died. Anne Hathaway's Cottage, which is really a substantial farmhouse, is over at Shottery, a mile westwards, an amiable black-and-white village mercifully untroubled by its publicity.

We get the best out of Stratford if we are playgoers. The appearance of the huge brick Memorial Theatre on the river-bank is now taken for granted. It has mellowed, and no one talks about it as a factory, a favourite cry in that cold spring of 1932 when the building shocked traditionalists. It replaced the sham-antique— burned to a shell during March, 1926—to which F. R. (Sir Frank) Benson, the Shakespearean of the sunrise mind, had given international fame. There are few happier experiences than to hear a play in the Memorial Theatre on one of those very calm June nights when Stratford seems as still as Hermione on her pedestal; during the interval to watch the Avon sparkling beside the theatre walls; and, after the play is over, to come out into an air scattered with balm.

Everyone will find a personal reason for loving the place. I choose the sight of the Guild Chapel when the moon is full and the shadows like Indian ink; the serenity of the church which has other beauties than the unfortunate Shakespeare Bust—look especially for the Clopton Chapel; the exterior of Hall's Croft (where one of Shakespeare's daughters lived); the tangled, spangled Knott Garden of New Place; and the grey lunge of Clopton Bridge where the wallflowers grow.

For all its inevitable trade in Shakespeare souvenirs, Stratford-upon-Avon is pleasant and welcoming. It is much the best place from which to visit the villages of the Shakespeare Country. Most people begin—and it is as good a way as any other—by seeing the eight villages of the apocryphal rhyme which Shakespeare is said to have tossed off when he woke under a crab-tree after a drunken night at Bidford. He had drunk, he said (or we are told that he said), with

> *Piping Pebworth, Dancing Marston,*
> *Haunted Hillborough, Hungry Grafton,*
> *Dodging Exhall, Papist Wixford,*
> *Beggarly Broom, and Drunken Bidford.*

None of these villages is in any special way a show-piece, but if we want to get the true atmosphere of the Avon country, that atmosphere which, as I have said, is like a long hot summer's day, we can do no better than wander among the tree-embroidered lanes and quilted, ample fields. I know of nothing gentler, more wholly English. There are various things to see: for example, a medieval bridge at Bidford and an ancient church at Wixford. My own favourite Shakespeare villages are to the north and north-east of Stratford. One is Snitterfield, from which Shakespeare's grandfather came, and which is on an upland, one of the few places round here I think of always in a pale February sun. An even quieter place is Hampton Lucy by the mansion of Charlecote. This vast Elizabethan house, shaped like a letter E and standing in a deer-park, has the grave courtliness of its period. We know as we see it, and certainly as we read Sir Thomas Lucy's epitaph upon his wife, that there can have been no connexion here with the "Justice Shallow" of the deer-poaching story, another of those Shakespeare legends it is better to forget.

To stay in Stratford for long is to become a collector of villages. There is Wilmcote which has Mary Arden's cottage, the home of Shakespeare's mother: I suggest that you walk to it from Stratford beside the sweet peace of a disused canal inhabited only by swans. Most people will walk during an evening to Clifford Chambers, which was once in Gloucestershire. In the opposite direction, out towards Warwick, the marks made by the cannon of the Parliament during the Civil War show still on the church at Barford. And away in another direction yet we can reach Cleeve Prior, with its manor-house and clipped yews that represent the Twelve Apostles. Wherever we go, we come back at night to Stratford-upon-Avon and to the peace that settles on the town after dark.

NEW PLACE GARDEN AND NASH'S HOUSE

CERTAIN foundations in New Place Garden are all that remain of the house which Shakespeare bought in 1597. In the adjacent Great Garden—where stands the mulberry tree said to have been planted by the poet's own hand—Shakespeare may often have talked with Ben Jonson and Michael Drayton. Long years after, the great actors Garrick and Macklin came here to do reverence. New Place Museum houses a collection of local antiquities. Properly called Nash's House, it now forms part of the Shakespeare Birthplace Trust.

SHAKESPEARE'S BIRTHPLACE

WE ARE here on hallowed ground. In this house in Henley Street, Stratford, on 23 April, 1564, was born to John Shakespeare and Mary, his wife, William Shakespeare, the playwright. (The exact date has been questioned, but it seems certain that it was on or near the 23rd. In those days of high infant mortality baptism followed swiftly on birth, and, as the Parish Register shows, Shakespeare was baptized on the 26th. The circumstance that 23 April is St. George's Day makes it finely appropriate that England's national poet should have first seen the light thereon.) His father seems to have been a wool dealer and glover—Aubrey maintained he was a butcher, a view nowadays discounted—a burgess of some standing who was a Chamberlain of the Borough of Stratford for the year 1562-3. The birth room (*above*) shows, scratched with a diamond on the window-panes, the signatures of the great and not so great, pilgrims equally to this cradle of genius. Amongst them those of Scott and Carlyle may be deciphered. Among the exhibits in the museum and library are the only extant letter known to have been addressed to the poet—by Richard Quiney, the father of one of Shakespeare's sons-in-law—and copies of the First, Second, Third and Fourth Folio editions of his works. Of the hundred thousand or more people who visit the Birthplace in an average year, about a quarter, it is computed, come from the United States of America.

THE BIRTHPLACE GARDEN

AFTER signing the visitors' book in the Birthplace, the well-conducted pilgrim steps into the garden, flanked by the building which now contains the offices of the Birthplace Trust and the library and record room. It is truly an old English garden; most of the flowers would have been familiar to Shakespeare himself. The view of the house from the garden is a pleasing one, showing characteristic features of the architecture of the year, 1485, in which it was built. In the middle of the path (somewhat obscured in this picture by the lupins) may be seen the base of the fourteenth-century stone market-cross, which formerly stood in High Street. Stratford is rich in old buildings, of which High Street (*below*) shows some especially fine examples. The "Tudor House" at the corner of Ely Street dates from the very end of the sixteenth century. It was most judiciously restored in 1903. Fanciful carving on the storey-post should be noticed. Next door to it is the Garrick Inn—better seen, with its neighbour, Harvard House, distinguished by its white flagpole, on page 23.

HOLY TRINITY CHURCH, STRATFORD

THE parish church of Stratford is a fine cruciform structure, dating in part from the twelfth century, with additions in the Decorated and Perpendicular styles of the thirteenth to fifteenth centuries. The present spire is a much later addition. The chancel, in the Perpendicular style, is its most beautiful feature, but the great south window, called the American Window, is full of interest, whilst its most priceless possession—apart from the grave and memorial of the Bard—is the Register, containing the records of the Shakespeare family.

SHAKESPEARE'S GRAVE

IN THE sanctuary of Holy Trinity Church, distinguished by brass plates, are the graves of William Shakespeare; Anne, his wife; Susanna, his elder daughter; and her husband, John Hall. A fifth grave is that of Thomas Nash, who married the poet's granddaughter, Elizabeth Hall. Shakespeare's monument, on the north wall of the chancel, was erected within a few years of his death. The arched recess is surmounted by the arms of the poet, and the half-length figure, the work of a Southwark mason, is held to be a good likeness.

HALL'S CROFT

IN THE street called Old Town stands the lovely Tudor house in which lived Susanna Shakespeare and her husband, Dr. John Hall. Acquired in 1949 by the Shakespeare Birthplace Trust, it has since been restored and a number of the rooms arranged for exhibition, one of them as a Shakespeare information and publications room. The Falcon Hotel (*below*), in Chapel Street, a private house enlarged and converted into an inn about 1660, contains some interesting eighteenth-century painted glass, and a room panelled in oak which is said to have come from the poet's house, New Place, whose garden it overlooks.

ANCIENT STRATFORD

THIS is probably the most photographed range of buildings in Stratford. Originally the site of a chapel of an Augustinian fraternity, the Guild of the Holy Cross, founded in 1269, the Guild Chapel is of great historic interest. The present building dates back to 1450. In the oldest part, above the chancel arch, is a touchingly naïve mural painting of "The Day of Judgement." Adjoining the Chapel is the Grammar School, where, by well-established tradition, Shakespeare received his education and acquired his "small Latin and less Greek." The schoolroom is on the upper floor, the lower being the old Guild Hall. The desk at which the poet is reputed to have sat can now be seen in the Birthplace. Next to the Grammar School, the old almshouses of the Guild fulfil today their original function of providing homes for twenty-four old people. Striking features of the older parts of the town are the tall brick chimney-stacks, designed to carry sparks safely above the once thatched roofs.

GRAMMAR SCHOOL COURTYARD, STRATFORD

STRATFORD'S ancient Grammar School is usually referred to as King Edward's School, the allusion being to the patronage of Edward VI. The truth seems to have been that in 1553 Edward returned to the town the property confiscated by the Crown in 1547, at the suppression of the Guild, with a stipulation that the endowment should be used for charitable and other purposes. The actual foundation of the school was considerably earlier. The first benefaction recorded was in 1482, by one Thomas Jolyffe, a priest, of Stratford.

HARVARD HOUSE AND THE GARRICK INN

IN HIGH STREET stands Harvard House, in which lived Katherine Rogers, who in 1605 married Robert Harvard of Southwark. It was their son, John, who endowed Harvard University. In 1909 Mr. Edward Morris of Chicago purchased the house and presented it to the University, by whom it is now owned. It has been restored and now closely resembles its original appearance. The beautiful timbered front is notable, as is that of the adjoining Garrick Inn, dating from about 1600, which, with its twin gables and hanging sign, is among the finest of Stratford's many splendidly preserved Elizabethan and Jacobean inns.

STRATFORD'S MOP FAIR

IN THE list of England's popular carnivals, great and small, ranging from the Goose Fair at Nottingham—a six-day orgy of strenuous jollification—down to the Furry Dance at Helston, in Cornwall, Stratford's statute fair, the "Mop," takes an honoured place. It is among the oldest. Going back for perhaps six hundred years, it was old even in Shakespeare's day, and it still seems to preserve more of its traditional quality than do its chief rivals, some of which have of late assumed a standardized pattern, and show all too clearly that they belong to the mechanical age. The old dances are one such survival. Sam Bennett (*right, top*), who died in February, 1951, at the age of eighty-five, is here playing for the Morris dancing at what was his seventieth Mop. Sam, who came from Ilmington, was a well-known figure in the country round. His fiddle dated from about 1630—little more than a dozen years after the death of Shakespeare. Stratford's Mop —the origin of the name is a matter for speculation—is held on 12 October each year. About mid-morning the official opening takes place. Wearing his robes and chain of office, the Mayor, preceded by the Town Crier and the Mace Bearers, heads the procession through the main streets of the town, which are lined with the stalls and booths of the showmen (*left*). Originally it was probably a hiring fair, and this character it maintained until shortly before the end of the last century. In former times the chief attraction of the Mop was the roasting—eight whole oxen and eight pigs were basted on the turning spits, which, in the early hours of the day, were set up in the streets outside the principal inns (*right, bottom*). Cuts from the roast, sizzling hot, could be enjoyed for a shilling a plate. This carnivorous custom persisted, with one brief interval following the First World War, up to 1939, when it was finally ended by food rationing.

25

THE ENGLISH FOLK DANCE

FOR some years past the English Folk Dance Society—founded by the late Cecil Sharp,
well known for his collecting of folk songs of the Appalachian Mountains—has held an

FESTIVAL AT STRATFORD

annual festival at Stratford. Here a gay throng, wearing the traditional bright costumes, dances with the hobby-horse round the maypole—and sometimes in the streets of the town.

SHAKESPEARE MEMORIAL THEATRE

THE first Shakespeare Memorial Theatre, comprising a theatre, picture gallery and library, was opened in 1879. The architect was W. F. Unsworth, and the style was something currently described as "free Gothic." The theatre was utterly destroyed by fire in 1926—an event which drew from Bernard Shaw a characteristic telegram of congratulation. No time was lost in planning a successor. A competition, open to all British, American and Canadian architects, was organized by the Royal Institute of British Architects, the winning design being that of Miss Elisabeth Scott, a great-niece of Sir Gilbert Scott. The completed theatre was opened by the Duke of Windsor, then Prince of Wales, in 1932. Executed in brick, the building is designed on simple, functional lines. The cost, more than £200,000, was raised chiefly by public subscription. Since American contributions (including a munificent gift of £100,000 from Mr. Rockefeller) amounted to something over two-thirds of the total subscribed, the writer who referred to the theatre as being "part-owned by the American nation" was amply justified. There can be few theatres with a more attractive setting. In the intervals it is delightful to sip tea on a balcony overlooking the Avon, or stroll upon the terrace beside the water, listening to the whisper of the poplars and the gentle, liquid sounds of the stream. It seems appropriate that the dramas which first came to life in the Globe Theatre, by the Thames at Bankside, should here be played out, before an audience drawn from the four corners of the world, in another riverside theatre —in the poet's native place. As a result of alterations to the auditorium, the seating capacity, formerly about 1,200, has been increased. The seats are arranged so as to focus one's attention upon the stage, and, the decoration being in greys and reds, with the walls panelled in dark woods, there is an absence of distraction. The acoustics—thanks in great part to the suspended roof—are remarkably fine. In all the essentials the new Memorial Theatre may be held to be a most successful piece of work. Of course, there is inevitably some incongruity between its somewhat severe lines and the pseudo-Gothic of the adjoining library and picture gallery, which, with their contents, both escaped the fire of 1926.

28

THE SHAKESPEARE FESTIVAL

THE Shakespeare Festival, usually opening some time in March, offers each year a six or seven months' season, in the course of which the repertory company gives a selection of plays. In more than seventy seasons the Memorial Theatre has performed nearly all Shakespeare's dramatic works including *Pericles* (which does not appear in the First Folio) but so far omitting the awkward *Titus Andronicus*. The season of 1951 brought the presentation of a historical cycle. From time to time the Festival has had stormy passages to weather, and undoubtedly it has had its ups and downs, but the standard both of acting and production is now extremely high. Among the distinguished directors and producers—several of whom have been noted actors in their own right—who have been associated with the Festival, one may mention Sir Frank Benson, W. Bridges-Adams, Ben Iden Payne, Robert Atkins, Sir Barry Jackson, Theodore Komisarjevsky, and, of a younger school, Tyrone Guthrie, Peter Brook and Anthony Quayle. Our pictures illustrate recent productions of three representative plays: a comedy, *Much Ado About Nothing*; a tragedy, *King Lear*; and a history, *King Henry VIII*; the producers being John Gielgud, Anthony Quayle and Tyrone Guthrie. The Trial Scene from *Henry VIII* (*top, left*) shows Anthony Quayle as the King and Gwen Ffrangcon-Davies as the unhappy Queen Katharine; Lear and the Fool (*top, right*), shows John Gielgud as King Lear. At the bottom is a gay scene from *Much Ado About Nothing*, with Peggy Ashcroft as Beatrice and John Gielgud as Benedick. (It is interesting to recall that it was with a performance of this same comedy that, over seventy years ago, the first Memorial Theatre was inaugurated. As in the recent production, the chief parts were played by two leading stage personalities of that day: Helen Faucit and Barry Sullivan.) Recent alterations, the boarding over of the orchestra pit and consequent bringing forward of the stalls, with the curving round of the circle into side boxes, have created a greater feeling of intimacy. Although the stage equipment is equal to any demands, there is a growing movement towards simplicity rather than elaboration of scenic effect. After all, at Stratford, the play's the thing.

31

BY THE AVON

THE Memorial Theatre and the adjoining picture gallery and library (*left*) rise beyond the poplars in the attractive waterside gardens. The library is especially devoted to Shakespearean and theatrical literature, its collection of the former being naturally one of the most complete in existence. Facilities are granted to students engaged in research work. The picture gallery contains portraits of Shakespeare (including the famous Droeshout engraving), and paintings of scenes from the plays and of noted actors and actresses. Among the painters represented are Reynolds, Hoppner, Romney and Hogarth, and there is also Rivière's celebrated portrait of Frank Benson. On the staircase are stained-glass windows, including one representing "The Seven Ages of Man." Boating on the Avon makes an ideal relaxation from playgoing. Punts, canoes and rowing-boats can be hired near Clopton Bridge and by the Bancroft Gardens (*above*). In June a regatta is held.

PAGEANTRY IN STRATFORD'S

ON 23 APRIL the bells of Holy Trinity Church break on the morning air in a joyous peal; an auspicious opening to a day of celebrations. The public Birthday Luncheon, organized by the Shakespeare Club and held in the Conference Hall, is followed by the customary speeches from distinguished visitors. Then, just after three o'clock, comes the ceremony of the flags. The signal is given and, from the tall poles planted three abreast all down Bridge Street, the flags of the nations flutter bravely in the breeze. Later, the procession—

ANNUAL CELEBRATIONS

Mayor, townsfolk and visitors—forms up outside the Birthplace and, headed by the band, proceeds solemnly to the church, to place flowers on the poet's grave. Besides the Birthday Sunday procession to Holy Trinity for the Shakespeare sermon, there are the May Day revels, culminating in the crowning of the May Queen. The picture on this page shows yet another ceremonial crowning which plays a part in Stratford's pageantry—that of the Flower Queen at the annual flower show which is held usually in June or July.

ANNE HATHAWAY'S COTTAGE

ORIGINALLY called Hewlands Farm, the "cottage" is in reality a fair-sized house. With its neat thatch, latticed windows and black-and-white walls, it seems the embodiment of homely comfort and rustic charm. Here it was, according to tradition, that Shakespeare came to court Anne Hathaway, whom he married at nearby Luddington, although that distinction is also claimed by Temple Grafton. Close to the fireplace in the parlour is the high-backed wooden settle on which the couple may have whispered together; there is beside much furniture of Elizabethan date. The cottage is in the care of the Birthplace Trust.

AT SHOTTERY

THE charming village of Shottery, little more than a mile from Stratford, is a pleasant walk across the fields. The old Bell Inn, the church beside the Shottery Brook, and the pretty old English gardens of the cottages, combine to form a lovely picture. Long before Shakespeare came here a-wooing—since the middle of the fifteenth century, in fact—there have been Hathaways living at Shottery, and they are living in Stratford still. A profound peace lingers in the cool, flagged courtyard of the stone-fronted Shottery Manor. Inside, the hall is particularly fine, with massive timbers and raftered roof of the hammerbeam variety.

"DRUNKEN BIDFORD"

IF HALF the stories which have grown up around the old rhyme, quoted on page 12, are true, "Drunken Bidford" saw Shakespeare in his most recklessly convivial mood. The scene of his potations was this old stone building with the moss-grown roof (*left*). In the poet's day it was the Falcon Inn, frequented by local topers whose capacity for ale rivalled that of Falstaff for sack. Bidford stands on the site of a Saxon settlement, established close beside a ford on the Avon believed to have been used by the Romans. Its fifteenth-century stone bridge of eight arches (*above*) is one of the finest in Warwickshire. The church, much restored in the last century, has some fine stained glass and a square, battlemented tower.

WELFORD-ON-AVON

WELFORD, the next village up the Avon from Bidford, is celebrated as one of the few villages which still keeps its maypole (*right*). And a formidable object it is— ribbon-painted, 70 feet high, and topped by a weathercock. It marks the old boundary between the counties of Warwickshire and Gloucestershire. The Avon here is very beautiful, and the long street of timber and thatched cottages (*below*), sloping down to the river, can hardly be surpassed for charm in all this countryside, rich as it is in villages of charm and character. Its name, Boat Lane, recalls the time when boats used to be drawn up on the strand at its foot. Besides its Norman church, Welford possesses an old water-mill, still working, and a rough-hewn Tudor lychgate, which is much painted by artists. The famous inn, "The Four Alls," stands on the Stratford road.

"PAPIST WIXFORD"

WIXFORD is a tiny village on the Arrow, a tributary of the Avon and a popular angling stream. The appellation "papist" probably springs from the circumstance that for five hundred years the village belonged to Evesham Abbey. Its old church (*above*), with its modest belfry tower, contains fine monuments of the fifteenth and sixteenth centuries. Near Wixford is the fifteenth-century Moor Hall, at one time surrounded by a moat. A few miles east of Stratford is Barford, where the road from Kineton to Warwick crosses the Avon by the fine stone bridge pictured opposite. (Note the missing capstone.) Barford lies in the brick country, but the village is still a pleasant one. Its chief claim to fame is as the home of Joseph Arch, the first agricultural labourer to enter Parliament. He is commemorated by a simple tablet. The tower of the church bears the marks of gunfire from the Civil War.

WILMCOTE—MARY ARDEN'S COTTAGE

A PLEASANT stroll of three miles along the banks of the reed-grown canal from Stratford brings one to Wilmcote and the house in which lived Mary Arden, Shakespeare's mother. With its lovely exterior and its rooms full of solid furniture, wrought, like the timbers of the house, from the mighty oaks of Arden, the old Tudor farmhouse is in itself worthy of its fame. It still has its square dovecote, with holes for more than 650 birds. The out-buildings behind the house contain a fine collection of ancient agricultural implements.

HAMPTON LUCY MILL

THE old mill on the Avon makes a pretty corner in Hampton Lucy, itself a village of great charm. Formerly called Bishops Hampton, it was for centuries in the ownership of the Bishops of Worcester. Its present name derives from the Lucys of Charlecote, to which family it came in the mid-sixteenth century. It is to a Lucy also, the Rev. John Lucy, that the village owes its handsome church in the Decorated style. Dating from the time of George IV and designed by Thomas Rickman, it is an early example of the Gothic revival.

ROMANTIC CHARLECOTE

STANDING in a stately park, with deer and a flock of Spanish sheep, Charlecote is a glorious example of a Tudor mansion house, dating from 1558. Its plan, in the form of an E (apparent in the *top*, *left*, picture), is generally explained as a compliment to the Queen, common enough in Elizabethan times; it is also, however, an admirable alternative to the "courtyard" plan, for securing ample air and light. The red-brick Tudor gatehouse (*seen above*) has remained unaltered since Shakespeare's day. It was in the Great Hall that the poet is said to have been haled before Sir Thomas Lucy, after a deer-stealing episode—one of the more unreliable of the Shakespeare legends. In 1945 the house and park of 228 acres were given to the National Trust. A corner of attractive Charlecote village is shown opposite (*bottom*).

THE old style and the new are vividly contrasted in the two pictures on the left. Years ago it was the flashing sickle which reaped the golden grain, but Warwickshire claims today to have the most highly mechanized agriculture in England. The great implement manufacturers of Coventry and Birmingham naturally regard the county as a convenient trial ground for all the latest developments and improvements in farm machinery. The large size, too, of the Warwickshire fields —large, that is, by comparison with those of some English counties—makes the use of modern machinery thoroughly practical. Although much of its acreage is permanent pasture, rich soil and a favourable climate make certain parts of the county ideal for grain growing. And, being in such close proximity, the large manufacturing towns of the Midlands provide a fine market, making dairy-

WARWICKSHIRE

farming and fruit- and vegetable-growing extremely profitable. The boys (*top, right*) are helping to gather the potato crop near Hampton Lucy. The neatly stooked cornfield (*bottom, centre*) is at Wellesbourne —a village which a good many years ago took a leading part in the movement for improving the conditions of agricultural workers. Fruit crops are often gathered by teams of itinerant pickers who travel from farm to farm, being paid on a contract basis. They work with a furious speed and a robot-like efficiency which allow small room either for aesthetic satisfaction or any savouring of the joys of husbandry. The picture here (*bottom, right*) shows workers of a very different type. The attractiveness of these fair pickers is not more evident than the enjoyment which they are taking in their task. This high-hedged field near Bidford-on-Avon is bearing a bountiful crop of raspberries.

BELL TOWER, EVESHAM

ALL that remains of the former Benedictine Abbey of Evesham is this superb example of late Perpendicular work, said to be the last medieval building of any importance executed in England by monk-builders. Abbot Lichfield completed the tower only a few years before the Dissolution of the Abbey in 1539, when all the earlier buildings were destroyed.

The Vale of Evesham

O pastoral heart of England! like a psalm
Of green days telling with a quiet beat . . .

THE author of those lines was the Cornishman, A. T. (Sir Arthur) Quiller-Couch, and he wrote them in his poem "Upon Eckington Bridge, River Avon." "Q" celebrated the Shakespeare Country with affection in a book upon the Warwickshire Avon, as well as in his *True Tilda*, where we sail for a few pages upon the Stratford-upon-Avon Canal, now long disused. We think first of the Eckington poem. It is hard now to see the name without repeating the queerly summoning lines:

Man shall outlast his battles. They have swept
Avon from Naseby Field to Severn Ham;
And Evesham's dedicated stones have stepp'd
Down to the dust with Montfort's oriflamme. . . .

I suppose that Evesham, twelve miles from Stratford, is thought of today not for its battle but for its market ("very celebrate," said Leland four hundred years ago); for spring blossom, when the vale seems to rise like Aphrodite from the foam; for the magpie-hued villages; or for the sight of Bredon Hill where Housman's pair "of a Sunday morning . . . would lie and see the coloured counties." These are coloured counties indeed. Only a few miles away are the warm, luminous, pearly golden-greys of Cotswold stone on the "high wild hills" (Shakespeare's term); but the Evesham vale is, like true middle England, a place of tree and meadow and park, a living embroidery of many shades of green, of silver, pink, gold, black-and-white. Nothing could well be calmer than the vale. It may seem perverse to think here of the clang of battle; but, as upon Edge Hill, we cannot forget the sound of civil war. It was a much earlier fight than Edge Hill, nearly four hundred years earlier, in the hot summer of 1265, when the army of the prince who was to be Edward I met the army of the great rebel baron Simon de Montfort, defeated it, and slew the leader. De Montfort had known that so the battle would end. At sunrise that morning, on climbing the Evesham bell-tower (not the present one) and seeing how the enemy was placed, he had cried: "May God have mercy on our souls, for our bodies are theirs."

It is strange how one is haunted by the "murder of Evesham, for battle none it was," the phrase used by the monk, Robert of Gloucester. With its fine churches and its shining river, Evesham is a jewel among English market-towns. It does not parade its history, and yet that hangs in the air. Those who are not historically minded can always celebrate the plum. We can call Pershore, six miles below Evesham, the plum of its area. The discerning Thomas Burke said well when he observed that although England was strewn with the "grey lace of Abbey remains," the Pershore plum remained "a thing unique . . . lovely and excellent in birth, in maturity, and in all phases between." Agreed; but no one can linger in Pershore without admiring the Abbey Church with its exquisite lantern. The villages that in and round the vale we shall remember best are perhaps Cropthorne, with its uncommon church; Offenham, among the orchards and by the willowed river; Elmley Castle, with its benign village square, upon Bredon slope; black-and-white Norton; Fladbury, Wyre. This will become a catalogue. All I can say is that every village in the list has that air of permanence so typical of this part of England where nothing, we feel, is fly-by-night, but all is rooted, firm, heart-of-oak.

We are near Cotswold; and no one will refrain from going across to Broadway at the foot of its sheer hill, a descent that offers fantastic views across the plain. Humphrey Pakington has called Broadway a Cotswold village that has slipped down the hill into Worcestershire. True; and it is a lovely village, though it is like a well-known beauty too conscious of itself and forever looking into the glass. For all that, it is a delight and we admire the golden-grey of its stone houses and forget the superficial glaze of sophistication. Madame de Navarro, who once lived there at Court Farm, was the American actress, Mary Anderson. In 1885 she made her début as Rosalind on the stage of the Shakespeare Memorial Theatre at Stratford-upon-Avon, and two of the three terracotta panels outside the Memorial Library there—those that illustrate scenes from *As You Like It* and *Hamlet*—Mary Anderson gave in memory of a great night. Her Orlando, a virile young actor who had been on the stage for eleven years, was Johnston Forbes-Robertson; a stuffed stag used in the Arden scenes came from Charlecote Park; and, so historians say gravely, even Audrey's turnip (not that the audience could have troubled about it) came from the garden of Anne Hathaway's Cottage at Shottery. The Rosalind was a triumph: the applause reached Mary Anderson, then just twenty-six, as a birthday gift. She is a radiant ghost to think of at Broadway.

Michael Drayton should have the last word about the Evesham vale:

Great Evesham's fertile Gleabe, what tongue hath not extolled?
As though to her alone belonged the Garbe of Gold.

The "Garbe of Gold." That is the word, and must always be whether you look down from above Broadway or from Bredon, whether you are in the mood for orchard tranquillity or for a battle-piece, for viewing the present serene and settled land, or for restoring it in the mind to its abbey-and-castle-guarded wildness.

BETWEEN AVON AND COTSWOLD

THIS scene, near Broadway, illustrates the meeting-place of two ways of livelihood. For here, at the foot of the Cotswolds, the Vale of Evesham begins. It was from the Cotswold sheep that the medieval wool merchants built the warm stone towns, with their superb churches. From pears, plums and apples has come the wealth of "Evesham's fertile Gleabe."

53

HISTORIC EVESHAM

EVESHAM is a veritable gallery of English architecture, showing examples of every style from Norman times to the present. Fine Georgian houses abound, but the eye is perhaps more surely taken by the lovely half-timbered buildings in the black-and-white, or "magpie," style. The most striking of these, the Booth Hall, graces the Market Place (*above*), in which the town stocks are still to be seen. A covered market occupied the lower floor of the Hall, town meetings being held in the upper storey; but in Tudor times the growing business of the town made the need for more adequate quarters urgent, and the present Guildhall was built. Evesham's importance as a market town—capital of the fertile Vale— is attested by the number of picturesque old inns. Abbot Reginald's Gateway (*left*) incorporates an old arch, dating from Norman times, a fragment of the former Abbey. In All Saints' Church, close to the Gateway, lie the remains of Abbot Lichfield, builder of the Bell Tower pictured on page 50. The nearby church of St. Laurence attracted pilgrims in thousands to the shrine of Simon de Montfort, who fell at the Battle of Evesham.

NEAR EVESHAM

AT MIDDLE LITTLETON, midway between Evesham and Bidford-on-Avon, is this superb group of fourteenth-century tithe barn, church and manor-house (*left*). The great barn shows an enormous expanse of roof, alternately bulging and sagging, but still sound. The gable end, which to the uninitiated looks as if it had been loopholed for defence, shows also the holes which make the barn virtually a pigeon-cote. Built in 1376, it is surpassed in age by the church, much of which is Early English, whilst the manor-house is a mere parvenu, being Elizabethan. Wickhamford (*bottom, left*), a few miles south of the Littletons, forms an interesting link with the Washingtons. In this gracious black-and-white manor-house lived Penelope Washington, whose mother married one of the Sandys family, the local squires. Penelope lies in the church, under a tablet engraved with the Washington arms. The ferry (*below*) crosses the Avon at Hampton, now practically a suburb of Evesham. The river is here an ample stream, most popular for fishing, boating and sailing.

RUSTIC CROPTHORNE

CROPTHORNE'S long main street of thatched, half-timbered cottages runs close to the Avon. Sweetly embowered in orchards, the village has moved many to describe it as the prettiest in England. Its fine church shows the building styles of five successive centuries, including a good deal of solid Norman work. And it may well be older still, for in Georgian times there was unearthed a cross head of the eleventh century, ornamented with the Greek key pattern, and showing no trace of the Celtic influence which was widespread at that time. The village is connected with Fladbury by the Jubilee Bridge over the Avon. This was the first English river to be adapted for navigation by artificial means. Weirs such as this one (*below*) near Cropthorne play an important part in controlling the level of the water.

FLADBURY FERRY

AT FLADBURY, not far from Evesham, this serviceable, if primitive, ferry is in regular use.
(It may be compared with the one at Hampton, pictured on page 57.) Away from main
roads, Fladbury is a haunt of ancient peace, with an old inn and a Queen Anne rectory. Its
water-mill, recorded in Domesday Book, was active as lately as 1930. The village retains its
fifteenth-century tithe barn, and the ancient church treasures some medieval stained glass.

PERSHORE ABBEY

FOUNDED in 689 by Oswald, nephew of Ethelred of Mercia, the Abbey of Pershore came later under the rule of the Benedictines. At the Dissolution the townsfolk, showing unusually acute judgment, retained for parish use not the Norman nave—which was promptly demolished—but the choir and transepts only. The finest features of the Abbey as it stands today are the Early English choir and the grand, Decorated lantern tower. (The pinnacles are a late-Victorian addition and would be better away.) The pear-blossom in the foreground of the picture recalls Housman's line, "the pear stood high and snowed." It recalls, too, the origin of the name Pershore, said to derive from pears. (It is written "Parshar" in old documents.) But Pershore has long been renowned not for pears but for the plum to which it has given its name. The market town for a rich agricultural area, it has fine old coaching inns and is known for its horse and cattle fairs. Pershore's mellow old bridge over the Avon (*below*) is relieved of traffic nowadays by the modern bridge built beside it.

THE Vale of Evesham is one of the gardens of England. See it in springtime, from some little hill rising like an island out of a sea of orchards with clouds of plum blossom drifting across it, the ground between the fruit trees a rich carpet of daffodils and wallflowers. Or, walking softly upon this carpet, catch a glimpse of some soaring pile—the Bell Tower at Evesham or Pershore's tall lantern—framed in the sprays of blossom. In the Middle Ages, apples—mostly grown for cider— were the principal crop; and there were large vineyards, extolled by William of Malmesbury in the twelfth century. Later, during the eighteenth century, the craze for the latest novelty, the strawberry, led to the orchards suffering grave neglect. The trees were crowded together, un-

tended, molested by cattle, abandoned to decay. How different from the modern orchard, tended with unceasing care, its trees sprayed and "ringed" against pests, root-pruned and pruned for shape, with steady replacement of the poorer stock! The two children (*left*) are gathering daffodils beneath a canopy of plum blossom; and the delicate filagree of the spring blossom (*right*) contrasts with the massive lines of the powerful draught-horses. The picture below shows Victoria plums being picked. The fruit is sorted and packed on the spot, ready for market in Evesham, where there are also canning, bottling and pulping factories. Tomatoes are largely grown, under glass, whilst Evesham asparagus, served in the local hotels, is considered a rare delicacy.

ECKINGTON BRIDGE

A FEW miles south of Pershore, where the Avon winds like a silver skein through the meadows, stands the lovely Eckington Bridge, the subject of a poem by Quiller-Couch. It is a very fine example of a late sixteenth- or early seventeenth-century stone bridge, fascinating in its unsymmetrical shape. The colour of the bridge, a rosy sandstone, forms a delicate harmony with the yellow of the spring flowers and the greenish blue of the water. In Eckington village the church is noted for its Norman west doorway, old glass and monuments.

INLAND WATERWAYS

NAVIGATION rights on the Lower Avon have been acquired by the Lower Avon Navigation Trust, and many thousands of pounds are being expended on a scheme which involves the cleaning out of the accumulated weed and silt and the repairing and improving of the locks. This view of Strensham Lock, near Eckington, was taken before work started on the scheme, which when completed will render a long stretch of the river navigable for the first time for seventy years and enable barges to leave the Severn at Tewkesbury and proceed right up to Evesham. Samuel Butler, the satirist, was born at Strensham.

IN BREDON'S SHADE

NOT far from the village of Eckington, lying snugly in a fold of Bredon Hill and sheltered by magnificent timber, is Woollas Hall (*above*). Dating from the early seventeenth century, it is a well-preserved example of English domestic architecture of the time when the somewhat Spartan living conditions of earlier days were giving place to more modern ideas of comfort. Its great hall has a finely carved screen and a musicians' gallery. The view from the ferry over the Avon at Twyning is of the essence of rural England. In the background rises Bredon Hill and, close at hand, with church, hall and tithe barn, is the village of Bredon. The tithe barn (*left*) dates from the fourteenth century and ranks as the second largest in England. A special feature is the outside stone staircase, sheltered by overhanging eaves, and the little warden's chamber over one of the porches.

66

BREDON HILL

BREDON HILL rises to a height of 960 feet. Its crest is crowned by Kemerton Camp, a British stronghold later used by the Romans. Inside the ramparts lies the Bambury Stone (*right*), a huge block shaped like a boat. From remains which have been found it seems likely that it was used as an altar stone. At the foot of the hill lies the village of Bredon (*pictured below*), the site, more than a thousand years ago, of a monastery of which no traces now remain. The church, dedicated to St. Giles, dates from the twelfth century, with additions of the thirteenth and fourteenth centuries and with a slender spire of still later date. In it is buried Thomas Copley, associated with Walter Raleigh in the founding of Virginia, and Giles Reed who endowed the village almshouses.

VIEW FROM BREDON HILL TOWARDS THE COTSWOLDS

THE BELLS THAT SOUND ON BREDON

ANOTHER charming village lying under the shelter of Bredon Hill is Overbury, known for its silk mills, which are powered by a water-wheel. The church, with a characteristic tower, is a Norman foundation, the nave showing a series of massive arches. The finely carved font is also Norman. Close by, Overbury Court stands on the rising slope of the hill, with a pretty garden bounded by neatly clipped hedges and limestone walls. Replacing an earlier house, its graceful Georgian lines seem to contradict its nineteenth-century origin.

TIMBER AND THATCH

A FEW miles south of Pershore, where the slope of Bredon Hill is beginning to rise above the Avon, as it curves in a great bow past Nafford Lock, is the village of Great Comberton. The squat, battlemented tower of its little church (*right*) stands, like that of Overbury, on a Norman foundation. Great Comberton possesses two notable dove-cots; one, built of mellow brick with a gabled roof, must surely be among the biggest in England. The picturesqueness of Little Comberton (*below*) seems almost excessive. Its church, again Norman, is similar in general appearance to that of its greater namesake, and has a fine oak door, dated 1639. Close at hand is a lovely black-and-white manor-house, which boasts a massive, round dove-cot, one of the finest of all the ninety odd dove-cots in Worcestershire.

ELMLEY CASTLE

ELMLEY CASTLE, one of the many half-timbered villages which lie in the shadow of Bredon Hill, takes its name from a once-strong castle of the Beauchamps. Falling into ruin, the castle became little more than a quarry for building materials. The old antiquary, Leland, mentions that stones taken from it were used in the repair of Pershore Bridge. The church, dating back to the Normans, contains some good monuments, including the beautiful and elaborately carved memorials to the Savage family. The Queen Elizabeth Inn is one of the many which claim to have given hospitality to that much-travelled queen.

CHILDS WICKHAM

A LITTLE way out of Broadway on the old road to Pershore lies Childs Wickham, the scene
of this charming combination. The slender spire of the church (somewhat similar to
Bredon's) is unusual in South Worcestershire. Many English villages retain their ancient
crosses, a great number of them unfortunately headless. Childs Wickham's wayside cross
is interesting in that the shaft is fourteenth- or fifteenth-century work, whilst the head is
much later. It dates probably from Stuart times. The adjacent inn is of the same period.

BROADWAY

BROADWAY, sometimes described as the only Cotswold village in Worcestershire, is very much a show place. Some, indeed, have complained that it flaunts its charms with too self-conscious an air. The long, grass-bordered street, sloping up towards the hills, is of ample width to set off to perfection the beautiful stone-built houses, mostly of the fifteenth and sixteenth centuries. The Lygon Arms, dating from the seventeenth century, is a famous hostelry. The Abbot's Grange, now a hotel, dates from the fourteenth century. Well-known houses include Court Farm, where lived Mary Anderson, the popular Shakespearean actress, the Prior's Manse, Tudor House and Picton House (*above*). Fish Hill, Broadway, over a thousand feet high, is crowned by the Beacon Tower (*left*), built as a viewpoint by the Earl of Coventry in 1800. It was actually lived in for a time by William Morris.

THE COLOURED COUNTIES

IT WAS, of course, from Bredon Hill that Housman's ill-starred lovers beheld "the coloured counties," but the view from Fish Hill, Broadway, is very similar, and even more extensive. It is said that in good weather no fewer than fourteen counties may be seen. In the picture below, the Vale of Evesham lies outspread like a carpet of pastel shades. The ridge running out on the right is Bredon Hill, whilst Cleeve Hill, the south-westerly spur of the Cotswolds, rises on the left. Peering over the shoulder of Bredon are the Malvern Hills and, lightly etched on the horizon, the Black Mountains of Monmouthshire and the tangled hills of Wales.

FOSSE WAY AT ETTINGTON

This ancient trackway, metalled by the Romans as a frontier road about the year 46, runs straight across Warwickshire. Here, a few miles from Stratford, it is quite a road, but in parts it is now merely a field track. Running from the south-west coast to Lincoln, it enters the Shakespeare Country near Shipston, skirts Compton Verney and, passing a little east of Leamington, cuts Watling Street at the High Cross, nearly nine miles north of Rugby.

The Fosse Way

I F WE look at a map of the Shakespeare Country we find the Roman road called the Fosse Way cutting sharply and diagonally across the eastern quarter. This is the straight Roman road that connected Devon with Lincoln and the north. We can use it for one of our pointers in the Shakespeare Country: most of the features pictured in the following pages are to south or east of the old ridge road.

For myself, when I consider this area I am always on one of two heights: looking down on the twisted, finely moulded brick chimneys of Compton Wynyates, or else gazing from Edge Hill upon the old Civil War battlefield, scene of one of the fiercest fights in English history. In Compton Wynyates, which is away in the extreme south-east of the country below Edge Hill, the associations for the most part are restful. We reach the place down a road that meanders among trees and suddenly, on the right hand, opens out a view of the rose-coloured house of the Northampton family deep below us, the twist-and-twine of its roofs rising (as those who love Compton think) always in sunlight: an early Tudor manor-house of fantastic beauty, the creation of a romantic tale. The Roundheads captured it during the Civil War, but we do not otherwise find much fighting in its career.

The "blast of war" sounds much more clearly farther up on Edge Hill (the "loftie Edge") on the Warwickshire border of Oxfordshire. Here we can look right across the plain to the hills on the March of Wales; across the scene of which a seventeenth-century writer said: "The Meadowing Pastures therein [lie] with their green Mantle, one so embroidered with Flowers, that from Edge Hill we may see it as the Garden of God." Indeed; and yet here, just below the long Edge Hill ridge, took place one of the first battles of the Civil War, that Sunday afternoon encounter (23 October, 1642) when the armies of Charles I and the Parliament (under Essex) fought for three and a half hours an indecisive and bloody conflict. Five thousand were killed and wounded. Ghosts are still supposed to re-fight the battle under Edge Hill. It is a scene for haunting, this place of

> . . . *war, red war, 'twixt child and sire,*
> *Household and kith and kin,*
> *In the heart of a sleepy Midland shire*
> *With the harvest scarcely in.*

Standing there, we can imagine how, on the first Christmas Eve after the battle, Edge Hill shepherds heard all round them at night the roar of cannon and the shouting; and how, on the next night and for other witnesses, the same "hellish and prodigious armies" worked their will.

Here, in this corner of Warwickshire, history streams its banners and beats its drums. There is the little hill-slope market-town of Kineton into which Prince Rupert's charge drove the Roundheads until the narrow street was blocked with carriages and wagons. But here, too, is a peaceful, retired world of great houses and tranquil memories. We find the church tower of Brailes, which is called "the cathedral of the Feldon," the open or corn-growing country of Warwickshire; the Tysoe villages in the Vale of the Red Horse, so called because a horse was once cut in the reddish earth of a hillside; and the lake-charmed mansion of Compton Verney, an Adam building in an enchanted setting. Farther towards the north are such places as Gaydon; Harbury, with its brass to one Jane Wagstaffe, a lady of the manor:

> . . . *For death on yerthe shall reape and mowe, that life*
> *therein hath tylde and sowen,*
> *And liefe agayne shall springe and growe, where deathe*
> *hath reapt and mowen . . . ;*

and Ufton, with its church-tower on the hill-top.

Let me mention only two more places. The high-set, healthy town of Rugby, which comes by courtesy into the Shakespeare Country, is the home of the great public school that for many must mean *Tom Brown's School Days*, the headmastership of Dr. Arnold, and the famous Close. I like to recall that one of England's most eminent classical actors was educated at Rugby, William Charles Macready, of whom Tennyson wrote: "Thine is it that our drama did not die, Nor flicker down to brainless pantomime." Macready, in his old age, remembered Rugby days during the French invasion when the school had its corps of volunteers and the elder boys wore blue coats cuffed and collared with scarlet and exercised after school hours with heavy wooden swords. Macready, when at Rugby, resolved to become a lawyer; but even at school he appeared as Hamlet in the Closet scene.

Finally, we should notice, as our farthest limit, Sulgrave Manor, twenty odd miles eastward from Stratford and in Northamptonshire. This small manor-house was the home of the Washingtons. Laurence, who was twice Mayor of Northampton and who died in 1583, bought the property from Henry VIII in 1539; one hundred and seventeen years later, in 1656, his great-grandson, Colonel John Washington, left for Virginia to found Mount Vernon. Shakespeare, of Stratford-upon-Avon, had then been dead for only forty years. It is agreeable to recall that Sulgrave was bought in January, 1914, for £8,400 by a body called, most pleasantly, the British Committee for the Celebration of the Hundred Years' Peace between Great Britain and the United States.

APPRENTICES TO AN ANCIENT CRAFT

THATCHING a rick does not call for the finished art of the master roof-thatcher. Speed is of the essence of the contract, for it may often be a race against time before the rain comes down. These young men are taking part in a thatching competition. Ropes of plaited straw and split hazel wands, bent into long pegs, are used to secure the thatch in place, the ridge being reinforced with an extra layer. Long Itchington, where this photograph was taken, is noted as the birthplace of St. Wulstan (Wulfstan), Saxon Bishop of Worcester.

A WARWICKSHIRE VILLAGE

LYING in a peaceful hollow near Compton Verney, in one of the "combes" from which both place-names are thought to derive, is Combrook, a village unknown to fame. To reach it the visitor must turn aside from one of the quieter stretches of the Fosse Way, along a road skirting Compton Verney's park. Here is typical Feldon, undulating open agricultural country, once in marked contrast with the forested area to the north-west of the county.

COMPTON VERNEY HOUSE

CLOSE beside the Fosse Way, a mile or two from Kineton, stands Compton Verney. The ancestral home of the Verneys, built in the middle of the eighteenth century, was the work of those two great architects, Vanbrugh and Adam. The estate came to the Verney family in the reign of Henry V, and the present house replaced one erected by Sir Richard Verney three centuries earlier. Seen across the lake, the façade, in the Palladian (Italian Classic) style, strikes the authentic note of the urbane country seats which graced the Age of Elegance. The beautiful grounds, nearly a square mile in extent, were laid out by the famous Capability Brown, and can show some of the finest cedar trees in the country.

CHESTERTON WINDMILL

THE rolling uplands south-west of Leamington are grand riding country, much favoured by the Warwickshire Hunt. Perched on a windy height, a landmark for miles around, is the curious building seen at the left. Built as a gazebo, or look-out, for Sir Edward Peyto in 1632, its design is attributed, somewhat doubtfully, to Inigo Jones. The original roof was later turned into a revolving dome and, fitted with sails, the building became a windmill. In Chesterton's isolated church, near-by, the Peyto family is commemorated by several striking memorials. The finest, dated 1585, has the recumbent figures of Humphrey Peyto and Anna, his wife. The ornate tomb of Sir William Peyto is held to be the work of Nicholas Stone. Not far away, beside the Fosse Way, are the grass-grown remains of Chesterton Camp, established by the Romans to safeguard their line of communications along the Way.

THE FIELD OF EDGE HILL

RISING to a height of 716 feet, Edge Hill makes a grand vantage point. This picture shows the outlook to the north-west, in which direction the view extends, in clear weather, as far as the Wrekin, seventy miles away. On the right can be seen Radway Church, rising above the trees which mask the village—a charming place of thatched cottages gathered round a green and with the gabled Radway Grange, where Fielding wrote parts of *Tom Jones*. In the middle distance, three miles away, lies Kineton, a small market town of fine stone houses, with a church which dates from the early fourteenth century. The oldest portion is the splendid tower; the remainder of the church was rebuilt artistically in 1775. Over the level plain in the foreground ebbed and flowed the fighting in the bitter Battle of Edge Hill.

STATELY UPTON

LESS than a mile from Sunrising Hill is the late
seventeenth-century mansion called Upton
House. Built in the reign of William and Mary,
the front shows characteristic features of the
style of the period—a style halfway between the
chaste ornamentation of the Caroline period and
the comparative plainness of early Georgian—
notably in the stone chimney-stacks, the long
row of plain dormers in the roof and the sash
windows. In 1948 the second Viscount Bearsted
presented the house, with its contents and
grounds of thirty-two acres, to the National
Trust, with a generous endowment. It can now
be visited by the public, and shows a wonderful
collection of works of art. They include a fine set
of Brussels tapestries and a collection of Sèvres
porcelain and Chelsea figures. The principal
attraction, however, is undoubtedly the superb
display of nearly two hundred pictures, among
them masterpieces of the English and the
chief continental schools. In the grounds is
a charming avenue, shaded by venerable yews.

86

FROM SUNRISING HILL

THERE are no stone walls in the Warwickshire landscape. The fields, large and remarkably regular in shape, are bounded by long, straight hedges, mostly of low, quick-set type, with hawthorn trees at intervals. Scattered about here and there, singly or in groups, often growing to a prodigious size, is the noble elm—"the Warwickshire weed." This is the view from Sunrising Hill, looking north-west, in the direction of Stratford. In 1642, on Sunday, 23 October, this fair landscape witnessed a bloody conflict. The Royalist forces were drawn up with the slope of Edge Hill at their backs. Their centre was in the village of Radway, the right rested on the Kineton road, where it breasted the slope, whilst the left was guarded by Sunrising Hill. The Roundheads, under the command of Lord Essex, were approaching through Kineton, and fighting did not begin until early afternoon. Prince Rupert, leading the Royalist cavalry in a furious charge, threw back the two wings of the Parliamentary army, but its centre stood firm. When, after some hours of bitter but inconclusive fighting, night fell, more than five thousand dead and wounded were left on the field.

RADWAY TOWER, EDGE HILL

THIS grim, battlemented tower was erected on the topmost point of Edge Hill in 1750, from the designs of Sanderson Miller. Cleverly faked at the time to counterfeit age, it certainly looks the real thing now. Its site marks the spot on which Charles I is said to have raised his standard for the opening battle of the Civil War. Now a refreshment house, called the Castle Inn, the tower commands the magnificent panoramic view described on page 85.

A SAXON CHURCH

A LITTLE to the west of the Edge Hill escarpment, fair in the midst of the wide-spreading Vale of the Red Horse, lies Tredington, famous for its fine old church dating from the time of the Saxons; their work shows plainly in arch and window. The massive wooden door —still serviceable after four hundred years—tells a graphic story of the Civil War. It is pitted with the marks of bullets, several of which are still embedded and can actually be touched.

COMPTON WYNYATES

WHAT can be said at this date about Compton Wynyates—a house which is known to every historian, architect or lover of that which is old and beautiful? Simply that, however much the theme has been overworked, Compton Wynyates *is* a lovely house in a lovely setting. In a deep dingle, the sides of which were once clothed in vineyards—which fact may offer a clue to the derivation of the name—it lies at peace, the great trees rising around and above it. Perhaps the most striking aspect is the west front, with its great gateway bearing above it the arms of Edmund Compton, and the flanking gables, where brick and timber mingle delightfully; but the whole composition, with its twisted chimneys and oriel windows and the lovely rosy tint of its mellow brickwork, is enchanting. The estate has been in the hands of the Compton family for eight centuries, but the beginnings of the present mansion were about 1500. Growing outwards by degrees from the original central hall, the later additions have grouped themselves around the glorious quadrangle, which is over fifty feet square. Still partly surmounted by battlements—which at one time were augmented by a moat—the house remains a perfect specimen, the *locus classicus* of a great Tudor manor-house. The banqueting room, or great hall, has the original timbered roof of Henry VII's time, much fine wood panelling, and a minstrels' gallery. More fine panelling and a plaster ceiling of the seventeenth century embellish the dining-room, which is hung with family portraits. Of great interest is the priest's room. With three staircases its occupant had two extra chances of escaping when danger approached. The house accommodated four hundred Parliamentary soldiers for a period during the Civil War. Having captured the house, the troopers successfully repulsed a moonlight attempt by the Comptons to retake it. In the grounds are a stone dove-cot and the family chapel, rebuilt in 1663, at which date the Compton monuments, after being salvaged from the lake, into which Cromwell's troopers had unceremoniously thrown them, were reinstated. The topiary work in the garden is amazing. Compton Wynyates is one of the seats of the Marquis of Northampton.

90

THE BURTON DASSETT HILLS

EAST of Kineton, the Burton Dassett Hills look out across the Midland Plain to the chalk downs of the northern Chilterns, and give fine views over the Vale of the Red Horse and the battlefield of Edge Hill. On the crest of the hills stands this sixteenth-century beacon tower. Faggots would be piled behind the parapet and stacked to the desired height all round the sloping roof, creating, when fired, a blaze visible for miles around. The village of Avon Dassett (*below*), a pleasant place of old cottages off the main road, shelters in a hollow of the hills. Within its modern church lies the carved effigy of a thirteenth-century priest.

SULGRAVE MANOR

IT IS a pleasant drive of just under thirty miles from Stratford to Sulgrave. The manor-house, home of the Washington family for more than a hundred and twenty years, is now arranged as a Washington museum, and is under the care of the Sulgrave Manor Board. It is richly furnished in harmony with the fashions of Tudor days. Laurence Washington, twice Mayor of Northampton, whose grave is in Sulgrave Church, bought the property from Henry VIII in 1539 and built the house in which his descendants lived until the mid-seventeenth century. It was in 1656 that Colonel John Washington sailed for Virginia to found Mount Vernon. George Washington, first President of the United States, was the Colonel's great-grandson. The arms of the Washingtons, the "Stars and Stripes," are on the gable and can also be seen in the church.

RUGBY AND ITS FAMOUS SCHOOL

ALTHOUGH on the Avon, Rugby comes into the Shakespeare Country only by courtesy. However, Stratford, aside from its other attractions, is a fine touring centre; and few who stay there will fail to make the twenty-five-mile journey to Rugby to see the famous public school—immortalized in *Tom Brown's School Days*—with which have been associated so many notable Englishmen. Founded in 1567 and handsomely endowed by Lawrence Sheriff, a native of Rugby, it rose to eminence under the great Dr. Arnold (father of Matthew Arnold, the poet), headmaster from 1828 to 1842. Amongst other Rugby masters, three—Dr. Tait, Dr. Benson and Dr. Temple—became, successively, Archbishop of Canterbury. The fine Temple Speech Room commemorates the last-named. In the Chapel is Dr. Arnold's memorial, a simply inscribed slab beneath which he lies. Other memorials include those of Dean Stanley and the poet Rupert Brooke, a Rugby boy in every sense, for he was born in the town. To thousands the name Rugby suggests the code of football which was born on the School playing fields. In 1823 William Webb Ellis, disregarding all the rules, first took the ball in his arms and ran with it, so originating the distinctive feature of the Rugby game. His exploit is recorded on a tablet overlooking the Close. The market town of a rich agricultural area, Rugby has large engineering and electrical works.

THE NORTH WARWICKSHIRE

WARWICKSHIRE is certainly one of the best hunting counties in England. Here are hounds of the North Warwickshire Hunt at Hampton-on-the-Hill, near Warwick. Another well-known pack, the Warwickshire Hunt, is centred on Stratford, whence it is no great distance to the meets of the Heythrop, the Croome, the Worcestershire and the North Cotswold. A meet of the last-named hunt, at Broadway, is pictured on pages 74-5.

The Forest of Arden

THERE are few more romantic place-names in Britain than the Forest of Arden. No Warwickshire men, in discussion of the comedy of *As You Like It*, will listen to pedantic talk about the Ardennes and Lodge's comedy of *Rosalynde*. The place is Arden. They will not bother about the absence from Warwickshire of lioness and "green and gilded snake." To them Another Part of the Forest must always be in Warwickshire; that is as they like it: Rosalind, Orlando, Celia, Jaques and Touchstone for ever haunt the area that, according to Michael Drayton—a Warwickshire man and proud of it—is the county's heart.

> *Muse, first of Arden tell, whose foot-steps yet are found*
> *In her rough wood-lands more than any other ground*
> *That mighty Arden held even in her height of pride;*
> *Her one hand touching Trent, the other, Severn's side.*

It is extremely hard today to give any special boundaries to the old area of Arden, a wooded district (not a forest as we think of the word) which covered much of North Warwickshire. As with the spelling of Sam Weller's name, much depends on the "taste and fancy" of the speaker. Here we enlarge our Arden to take in places as far apart as Alcester, Studley and Coughton on the one hand, and, on the other, Kenilworth, Warwick and Leamington, and Stoneleigh. The use of the name should not be regarded as more than a way of delimiting a section to the north of the Shakespeare Country.

Henley-in-Arden to which we can go first, as it is rightly named, is a gentle, agreeable old town. Like the late W. H. Hutton, I have never been able on my visits to discover any of the "loose life" that in 1655 produced the following statement: "Usually heretofore there have been at Henley-in-Arden several unlawful meetings of idle and vain persons about this time of the year for erecting May Poles and May Bushes, and for using of Morris Dances and other heathenish and unlawful customs, the observation whereof tendeth to draw together a great concourse of loose people." Whatever may have happened then, it is now a serene place indeed.

There is much to look for in this part of the world: the old timbering of the Henley houses, the Norman church of Beaudesert, the even older church of Wootton Wawen. South-westwards are Coughton where, in Domesday, there was land for six ploughs and pasture for fifty swine, and where now we discover the superb Tudor gate-house of Coughton Court; and Alcester, a market-town that can go back to the Romans. River and meadow; manor, farm and cottage: that is the usual Warwickshire pattern. The most dramatic parts of Arden are those round the castles of Warwick and Kenilworth. I do not think the least imaginative visitor could keep calm about Warwick Castle. This is everything that a castle ought to be. Its towers rise, massy and impregnable, from a cliff above the Avon. It gives an impression of immense strength. Beauchamps, Nevilles and Dudleys have been seated there. Piers Gaveston was imprisoned by the "black dog of Arden" before his execution on Blacklow Hill in 1312; Warwick the King Maker ruled in this great fortress. It is medieval England in stone. The town, with its lovely Leycester Hospital and its dominating church of St. Mary (the casket of the Beauchamp Chapel within it), seems to be occupied by the castle's retainers.

While Warwick lives, Kenilworth is a majestic ruin. For most people it is the title of a Scott novel they do not read. It is time we returned to Scott. He is a superb story-teller; he makes Elizabethan Kenilworth live so vividly that, for all the obvious anachronisms, we can re-people the pile that Elizabeth granted to Robert Dudley. Not everyone can "feel" a castle. One fragment of weathered stone can be much like another. But Kenilworth, with its mighty Leicester Buildings, is something to fire any mind. And nothing is wrong with the romantic air of Guy's Cliffe, still one of the great mansions of Arden. Guy of Warwick, says the legend, lived here in a cave as a hermit after he had slain the Dun Cow of Dunsmore, that "monstrous wyld and cruell beast," won and deserted his wife, and behaved with the oddity proper to so cloudy and fabulous a figure. I prefer to remember that Sarah Siddons was for some months a lady's maid in the mansion of Guy's Cliffe, long before those terrifying days when, as the most famous actress in the land, she was apt to be a tragedienne off the stage as well as upon it.

Leamington Spa, among its trees, is amiable and demure after the knights in armour. In various parts of Arden there are the clipped yews of Packwood, recalling the Sermon on the Mount; at Meriden what is deemed to be the precise centre of England and Wales; and at Stoneleigh the ancestral home of the Leighs, once a Cistercian Abbey.

As I have said before, this Arden is "unmitigated England," even though we can never find in it a Rosalind, a Celia or a Jaques. No matter. If we are lucky, at least one Stratford-upon-Avon Festival in three should bring to us the voice of Charles the Wrestler as he answers Oliver's question, "Where will the old Duke live?" with that fine flare of speech:

> "*They say he is already in the forest of Arden, and a many merry men with him; and there they live like the old Robin Hood of England; they say many young gentlemen flock to him every day, and fleet the time carelessly as they did in the golden world.*"

LEYCESTER'S HOSPITAL, WARWICK

THESE fourteenth-century almshouses take their name from Queen Elizabeth's favourite, the Earl of Leicester. In 1571 the Earl gave money to endow a home for aged soldiers, and desired that Warwick's Guildhouse, as it then was, should be fitted up to accommodate twelve brethren and a master. This company the "hospital" maintains to this day. They still wear their traditional costumes of blue cloth with the original silver badges.

99

HENLEY-IN-ARDEN

WHAT a place is Henley-in-Arden! Expectations aroused by its romantic name are not disappointed by the glorious main street, lined by buildings of varied styles and fascinating irregularity. Many of them are half-timbered, with upper storeys which project far over the pavement. There is a thirteenth-century market cross (*left*), so slender that it needs these somewhat unsightly railings and bracers to keep it safe amid the hazards of modern traffic. There are ancient inns without number. The Parish Church has a square tower with a battlemented top, and dates from the fifteenth century. Next door stands the timbered Guildhall, built in 1448 by Ralph Boteler, whose arms are over the fireplace. Behind the Guildhall, overlooked by the church tower, is a delightful Dutch garden (*below*). Just across the river from the High Street is Beaudesert, with a lovely Norman church and, close by, the mound of a vanished Norman castle.

REVELRY IN ARDEN

THE timber fronts of the old houses provide a setting for Henley-in-Arden's annual carnival such as no stage scene or film set could hope to equal. Henley's junketings are proverbial. Indeed, in the middle of the seventeenth century its name became a by-word, so far were the townsfolk from taking their pleasures sadly. It was thought grave cause for scandal that "idle and vain persons" should set up the maypole and dance the morris.

CARL A. RUDISILL LIBRARY
LENOIR RHYNE COLLEGE

WOOTTON WAWEN AND ASTON CANTLOW

BETWEEN Henley-in-Arden and Alcester, along the valley of the little River Alne, lie these two villages, typical of those of the Forest of Arden. Wootton Wawen (*top*), just over two miles south of Henley, is charmingly situated among the great trees of Arden, with almshouses, hall and inn, and the River Alne expanding gently into Wootton Pool. The special glory of Wootton Wawen is its lovely church, a Saxon foundation, rich in interest and said to be the oldest in Warwickshire. This distant view reveals the delicate Perpendicular work of the nave and of the battlemented tower, fairly bristling with pinnacles ornamented with the most intricate crocketing. The sturdy Saxon work of its first builders is best seen in the four small arches by which the tower is supported. Besides its architectural riches, the church has all manner of other treasures. They include the fifteenth-century carved oak screen and pulpit, ancient muniment chests decorated with hoops, hinges and clasps of wrought iron, and several chained books. Among the tombs is one with the alabaster figure of a man in armour of the time of Henry V. Aston Cantlow (*bottom*) is a further two miles towards Alcester. Wilmcote is in the parish, and Snitterfield is only a few miles away. With the ruins of a castle, an old guildhouse—now divided into cottages—and a fine old church, its quiet yard shaded by yews, Aston Cantlow is full of interest. But its special claim to fame is that here, so it is believed, John Shakespeare of Snitterfield and Mary Arden of Wilmcote were married in 1557. From their union sprang William Shakespeare. Had the church no Shakespearean associations it would still merit attention. It is thought to date from about 1290, and has a carved font and much fine woodwork of the fifteenth century. The clock in the tower is said to be six hundred years old, and is still working. The building is one of great strength and may well have been used for defence. On the outer wall, below a window, can be seen what are presumed to be the marks of arrows. The name Cantlow is derived from the Cantelupe family, the village having been given to William de Cantelupe in the reign of King John.

ROMAN ALCESTER

ALCESTER, "the camp on the Alne," stands close to the important Roman road called Icknield Street. Many evidences of the Roman occupation have been discovered locally—coins, pottery and traces of the buildings of the camp. The old market-town is remarkably picturesque. Its medieval houses, mostly modernized inside, have happily retained their finely carved, timbered fronts. The seventeenth-century Town Hall (*above*) followed custom in housing a covered market. Malt Mill Lane (*above, left*) shows a fine range of cottages with overhanging upper storeys. The greater part of the church was rebuilt in the eighteenth century, but it retains a fine Early English tower. Coughton Court, now owned by the National Trust, lies about two miles north of Alcester. Prior to 1946 the estate had been held by the Throckmortons for over five hundred years. The present house (*left*) was built about 1500. It was at Coughton that the wives of some of the conspirators in the Gunpowder Plot waited anxiously for the result.

105

RIVER ARROW, NEAR ALCESTER

NEAR Alcester, the little River Arrow, a tributary of the Avon, is joined by the Alne. Close to the watersmeet, in a beautiful park of five hundred acres, stands Ragley Hall, seat of the Marquis of Hertford. Its situation is superb, and the Hall, of classical proportions, is made more impressive by the portico added early in the nineteenth century. Arrow Church is near-by and has a tower which is believed to have been designed by Horace Walpole.

THE HEART OF ENGLAND

AT MERIDEN, a village between Coventry and Hampton-in-Arden, stands the stone cross (*right*) which claims to mark the exact centre of England. (A vigorous counter-claim is put forward by Lillington—pictured on page 120—and there are other claimants to the honour.) On the village green is another memorial, an obelisk commemorating cyclists who fell in the Great War. Packington Hall, near Meriden, stands in a finely wooded park of seven hundred acres, containing several ornamental lakes. It is the scene of the ward-mote, or annual meeting, of the Woodmen of Arden, the oldest archery society in England. The picture below shows a contest in progress in the grounds, the Woodmen wearing their quaint ceremonial costume—bottle-green tailcoats with brass buttons, white nankeen trousers, and felt wideawakes.

MIGHTY KENILWORTH

IN ITS combination of romantic aspect, beauty of situation, extent of its remains and interest of its historical associations, Kenilworth stands unrivalled. (For its powerful "atmosphere" Scott's novel must take all due credit.) Mighty even in decay, few castles give a more vivid impression of the glory and the strength, the "drums and tramplings" of a bygone age. The castle's story goes back to the days of Henry I. It was largely extended in the reigns of King John and Richard II, and again, in Elizabethan times, by the Earl of Leicester. He built the gate-house (at the extreme left of this picture) and also the great block of buildings known by his name whose windows show gauntly at the right. The gate-house is in splendid repair, as—considering its age—is the keep, sole surviving portion of the original fortress. (It occupies the centre of the picture.) The fine block facing the keep contains the great hall, or banqueting chamber. Although without roof or floor, it still shows traces of its former magnificence and recalls the pomp with which Queen Elizabeth was entertained by Robert Dudley in 1575. Leicester's Barn is the name given to the lovely half-timbered range of stables partially seen to the right of the gate-house. In front of them, amid the fine trees which now shade the outer ward, are foundations of a chapel built by John of Gaunt, by whom also the great hall and apartments of state were erected. Since 1937 the castle has been in the possession of the nation, and much good work has been carried out by the Ministry of Works in removing ivy, strengthening walls and arresting decay.

IN KENILWORTH

IF TIME had unkindly swept the castle away, Kenilworth would still be worth visiting. The old houses opposite the castle entrance group themselves delightfully around Clinton (or Castle) Green (*above*). High Street, equally picturesque, leads down to St. Nicholas' Church, famous for its magnificent Norman doorway, probably transferred at the Dissolution from the Augustinian Priory founded in 1122 by Geoffrey de Clinton, the founder of Kenilworth Castle. The foundations of the Priory, with the substantial remains of the fourteenth-century gate-house and the porter's lodge, still exist close beside the church.

STONELEIGH-IN-ARDEN

STONELEIGH ABBEY, the residence of Lord Leigh, is one of the great houses of England. Little more than a mile from Kenilworth, it stands in a lovely park watered by the winding Avon. A Cistercian abbey was founded here by Henry II in 1154, and parts of the monastic buildings are incorporated in the mansion, which dates from 1710–20. The imposing west front (*seen above*) shows pilasters of the Ionic order, surmounted by a deep cornice and balustrade. Inside, the great staircase and the carved oak panelling are notable, whilst the salon, ornate with moulded plaster-work on walls and ceiling, is of almost regal magnificence. The gate-house of the old abbey, dating from 1349, remains in a fine state of preservation.

GUY'S CLIFFE

A LITTLE way north of Warwick, romantically situated beside the Avon, is the handsome late-Georgian mansion called Guy's Cliffe. Close by is the chapel, founded in 1416 by Richard Beauchamp, Earl of Warwick, in honour of the exploits of the legendary hero, Guy of Warwick. Returning from the Holy Land, after distinguishing himself in the Crusades, Guy determined to become a hermit and chose this quiet spot as his retreat. The cave in which he is supposed to have lived may be visited, and his statue, eight feet high, carved out of the solid rock, stands in the chapel. At Guy's Cliffe, it is interesting to recall, Sarah Siddons was for a time in service as a lady's maid. The most attractive view of the mansion (*right*) is obtained from the stone parapet of the old mill across the river. Popularly called the Saxon Mill, in allusion to its mention in Domesday Book, it is really of later date, although the old well (*left of the picture above*) may go back to Saxon times.

THE AVON AT WARWICK

A NOBLE stream must add immeasurably to the charms of any town. Here at Warwick the Avon, deploying several of its loveliest reaches, offers delectable riverside lawns on which to stroll or linger. From Castle Bridge one can take rowboat or punt, or cruise in one of the blunt-nosed motor craft, whilst, from the grassy banks, the angler watches the bobbing float. Bathers disport themselves in an open-air pool beside the Avon in St. Nicholas' Park.

ON PINNACLED ST. MARY'S

THE beautiful, pinnacled tower of St. Mary's Church, Warwick, commands a grand view. This picture is taken looking south-east, straight along Church Street and away over the flat open country in the direction of Whitnash and Harbury. At the end of the row of steep-pitched roofs is the classical Court House, built in 1730. Beyond, in Castle Street, the house with the half-timbered gable-end is one of several willed to charity by Thomas Oken, a rich mercer, in 1573. The battlements of the Castle show just above the trees, with Guy's Tower rising boldly to the left and partially obscuring the more famous Caesar's Tower.

WHERE KINGS WERE MADE—WARWICK

THIS view of the castle, taken from the bridge over the Avon at Warwick, is justly celebrated. Warwick Castle, in Scott's phrase, "uninjured by Time," combines the goodly stronghold of warlike barons with the stately apartments of a seventeenth-century great house. Of the older portions, Caesar's Tower, nearly a hundred and fifty feet high, and Guy's Tower, to

CASTLE AND THE RIVER AVON

its right, both date from the fourteenth century. The mansion, largely rebuilt in the seventeenth century, occupies the river frontage; the embattled wall connecting the series of towers encloses the inner court, entered through the massive gate-house. From 1449 to 1471, Richard Neville, better known as "Warwick the King Maker," lived in the castle.

PICTURESQUE SCENES

HAPPILY, some few of the most picturesque corners of Warwick survived the great fire of two hundred and fifty years ago. Mill Street (*above*) leads down from the Castle Lodge to the Avon. Its ancient red-roofed cottages display a fine variety of Tudor fronts. (Note also the attractive flight of steps.) St. Mary's Church (*top, left*) was a Saxon foundation; the crypt of its Norman successor remains. Of the splendid church built by the Beauchamps in the fourteenth century only the beautiful chancel (and the later Beauchamp Chapel) escaped the fire of 1694. The finest part of the rebuilt church is the impressive tower, 174 feet in over-all height, surmounted by crocketed stone pinnacles. As the Parish Church of Warwick, morning service is attended every Sunday by the Mayor and Corporation. Entered from the south transept by a finely carved doorway is the Beauchamp Chapel (*bottom, left*), which ranks with King's College Chapel, Cambridge, and the King Henry VII Chapel in Westminster Abbey as a supreme example of Perpendicular Gothic

IN MEDIEVAL WARWICK

architecture. Begun in 1443, it took more than twenty years to finish. It is a worthy memorial to the great noble, Richard Beauchamp, Earl of Warwick, governor of the dominions of King Henry VI in France and Normandy. He it was—representative of the secular power—who is remembered for the burning at Rouen of Joan of Arc. His effigy, superbly executed in bronze, lies on a great altar tomb. Even larger in size is the striking tomb of Robert Dudley, Earl of Leicester, the favourite of Queen Elizabeth. At one time Warwick was a walled town, but now the only remains of the twelfth-century walls are one or two fragments and the magnificent East and West Gates, between which stretches the chief thoroughfare of the town. The East Gate (*top, right*) is surmounted by St. Peter's Chapel, which dates from the time of Henry VI. The celebrated Warwick Vase (*bottom, right*), housed in a greenhouse in the Castle grounds, is attributed to the Greek sculptor Lysippus. This exquisitely carved marble vessel was found amid the ruins of Hadrian's villa at Tivoli.

119

MIDLAND ENGLAND

THE Midlands are rich in canals. The watersheds dividing the river basins are comparatively low, and the eighteenth century saw the growth of a great system of inland waterways. Pictured above are Hatton Locks on the Warwick and Birmingham Canal, part of the Grand Union system connecting London with Birmingham and the Potteries. A Royal Commission recommended in 1930 that more use should be made of the canals; and the Inland Waterways Association is adopting a vigorous policy for their repair and maintenance, and for popularizing transport by water. At Lillington, near Leamington, where the Kenilworth road diverges from the Rugby road, stands the Midland Oak (*left*), said to mark the centre of England. Lillington's title is challenged, however, by a number of other places, each claiming the distinction for itself.

VICTORIA BRIDGE, LEAMINGTON

SPA life at Leamington seems largely to revolve around this fine bridge over the Leam. At opposite ends of it stand the Parish Church and the Pump Room. Upstream, the Leam has gardens on both banks; Mill Gardens on the right and, opposite them, the Jephson Gardens. Downstream lie York Bridge and Victoria Park, with its riverside walks.

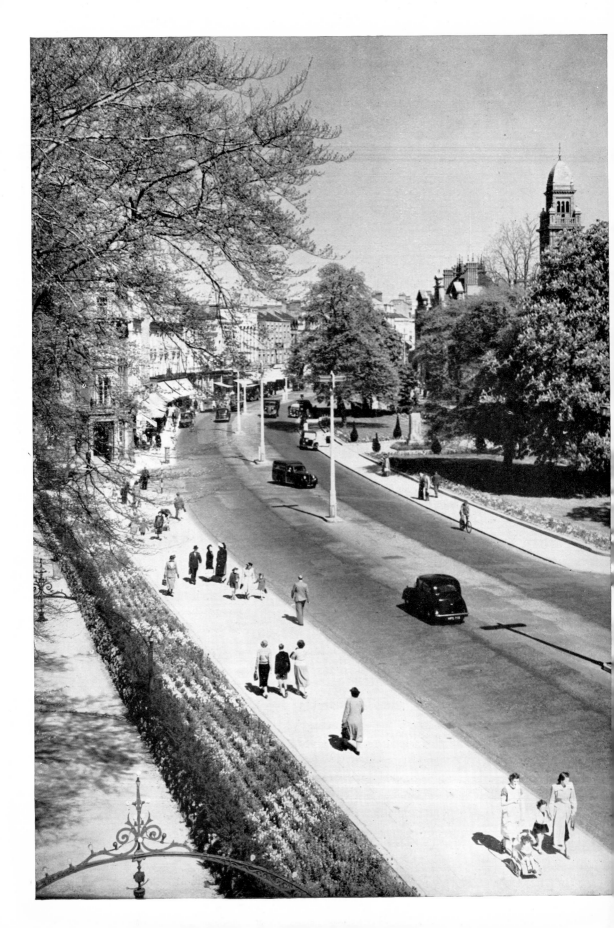

ROYAL LEAMINGTON SPA

WITH its clean, wide streets, bordered by trees, its parks and public gardens, and the little River Leam, which gives such pleasant waterside strolls, Leamington deserves its description of "The Garden Town." It is practically all the creation of the last hundred and fifty years. The curative properties of its waters were known long before, but it was only towards the end of the eighteenth century that the efforts of three men, William Abbots, James Bissett and Benjamin Satchwell, led to the spa becoming widely appreciated. The Pump Room and Baths were built in 1808. Dr. Thomas Jephson, whose statue adorns the gardens which bear his name, did much to raise the esteem in which Leamington's cure was held. Lower Parade (*left*) is the town's principal thoroughfare, with the tall campanile of the Town Hall overtopping its bordering trees; the Pump Room Gardens are on the left. In the opposite direction, beyond the Victoria Bridge is All Saints' Church (*above*), with an impressive modern tower, in the Decorated style. The Pump Room, on the right, is in the dignified Regency style of so many of the buildings in the town. Royal visitors to the baths have included George IV and Queen Victoria, the latter in 1830 when Princess Victoria. In 1838 she permitted the town to adopt the title of Royal Leamington Spa.

HIGHLIGHT of the farming year is the agricultural show. This picture (*above, left*) is of the Kenilworth Show, but a similar scene might be witnessed in any of a score of places throughout the county. In deciding between the nearly equal merits of hundreds of entries—frequently there will be more than fifty livestock classes—the judges have an exacting task. Apart from the livestock exhibits, there are the usual competitions in butter-making, cake-baking, dressed poultry, embroidery and handicrafts, while no programme is complete without its dog show. Working with hand clippers, an expert will take something like twelve minutes to shear a full-grown sheep. In this competition near Leamington (*above, right*), modern power-operated shears are being used. Ploughing

124

contests, whether part of the annual show or separate events, are always popular. The horses, with coats groomed to the texture of silk, traces polished and harness-ornaments burnished bright, make a fine spectacle. Horse ploughing, although naturally less speedy than tractor ploughing, is considered by some authorities to produce better results. A skilful ploughman can drive his furrows as straight as a machine. In most country districts the wheelwright still finds plenty to do. This craftsman at Barston (*right*) is seen fixing a spoke to the felloes of a cartwheel. Shrinking the iron tyre on to the outer rim is a highly skilled operation. The heated metal is hammered into shape on the wheel and then rapidly cooled down, the contraction ensuring a tight fit.

125

THE LEAMINGTON COUNTRY

THE countryside about Leamington is typical of rural Warwickshire in its quieter moods. There are a number of pretty villages, many half-timbered, and much first-class farming land. The scene pictured above is at Red House Farm, close to Leamington. Drawn by a tractor, a modern reaper and binder is harvesting a field of wheat. The machine drops off, at intervals, the sheaves which it has bound; later the harvesters will build them into stooks. The blossoming orchard seen at the right is at Bishop's Tachbrook. The village, lying some two miles south of Leamington, has an Early English church which, in addition to the monuments of the Wagstaffes, the local squires, contains also the graves of the Landors who lived hereabouts for many years. Walter Savage Landor, the poet and scholar, spent his childhood at Bishop's Tachbrook. He is commemorated by a tablet in the church.

INDEX TO PHOTOGRAPHS

ACKNOWLEDGEMENTS

The publishers are indebted to the following for permission to reproduce the pictures appearing on the pages indicated: Birmingham Gazette, Ltd., pages 24, 25 (top), and 125 (bottom); Aero Pictorial, Ltd., pages 28–9; Angus McBean, pages 30 and 31; Evesham Journal and Four Shires Advertiser, page 34; Sulgrave Manor Board, page 93.

First published 1951
Made and Printed in Great Britain by Odhams (Watford) Ltd., Watford
Copyright. T.751.R.